Put Feet To Your Dreams And Get Walking!

"Wisdom at a Glance"

By Jayne Lybrand

D1516209

Cover Photos: Ralph Holloway Photography
Hair Stylist: Jolene — and the entire Perfect "10" staff.

Printed in the United States of America
by Branch-Smith, Inc., Fort Worth, Texas

Dedication

To the "Pride of my life"
my inspiration
my loving daughter
Elizabeth
who has given of her very life and talents
to help us build our world
and for keeping me in line!

To my adoring mother
Ruby McHugh Brannon
whose prayers, positive attitude
and undying faith in God and me
keep me going!

To the memory of my dear father
Rev. J.D. Brannon
— who taught me I could do anything!
(within reason).

Acknowledgements

Dr. George Tade — for his editing assistance and listening ear—my Master teacher and mentor — Dr. Tade dreamed big dreams for me before my dreams could even walk!!!

Wilma Jean Tade — the other half of my life long support team — I love you for the many hours of listening and visiting me during my pain and joy!

Dr. Susan Blue — and family — whose constant friendship and care — always going that last mile — to teach me to smell the roses "while my sniffer still works!"

Dr. Ken Olson — my friend of many years — who first saw my uniqueness and urged me to quit my "real job" and speak full-time. He taught me to always "bet on me!"

Dr. Charles Kemp — whose guidance has helped me discover myself!

Dr. Richard S. Brannon — for his editing suggestions and most importantly — always being my brother when I need him most!

Sherry McKay — My dear friend who is always there — to motivate the motivator!

Poppa Roy and Moma Dorris Leverich — for their love and second home which has become my writing haven.

Robert Smith — for his staying on my case to finish this book!! Thanks for Cracking the Whip! It worked!!

Jan & Jim Batts and Family — for all the time and months of travel to help me get started on this book. Jan compiled my first "dress rehearsal" book! Thanks for making me finally do it myself!

Margaret Johnson — My Macintosh Plus Samaritan!

Minnie Capello, the "girls," and the entire "Suarez Family" — my guardian angels.

Jimmy Ferguson — who booked me first in the college market and showed me the great need for my services.

To the National Association for Campus Activities — whose organization has become like a family. Thank you for putting "feet" to my lecture career!

Joan Price — For helping me "unclutter my life" so I could write.

Marion Kjellander — for her positive love and nurturing kindness!

Bill and Beverly Brune — whose love and graciousness has kept me fed — both in body and soul!

Carolyn Deibel — especially for the care during the "tough times."

Dorothy Hamm — For the many years of believing in me and tackling the manuscript on the typewriter and new computer.

Virginia (Mother) Helvey and Family — for always being there!

To the entire Brannon and McHugh family — Thank you for your special love.

To the Birdville Independent School District — for teaching me from the first grade how to believe in my creative skills. Thank you for your continued loyalty.

To all the hundreds of colleges, corporations and conventions that have believed in me and requested this creation of my "Heart on Paper"!

To the media — for your interest and hard work that has resulted in allowing me to reach so many people!

Table of Contents

Author's Comments vii

Chapter 1
"Feardom of Speech" .1

Chapter 2
Love Relationships 5

Chapter 3
Why Not To Get Married! 11

Chapter 4
Failure Is A Dress Rehearsal for Success . .29

Chapter 5
Self-Esteem And Dealing With Our Fears .33

Chapter 6
Success Tips I Want To Tell You 43

Chapter 7
Parent Talk 61

Chapter 8
Kid Talk 69

Chapter 9
"Tapestry Living" 81

Put Feet To Your Dreams And Get Walking!

AUTHOR'S COMMENTS

I am the way I am because when I was growing up none of my toys had batteries!

The potential domain held by a fresh, new large cardboard box held visions in my eyes. I needed no curtains, furniture, carpet or colors. My mind's eye saw my cardboard shell fully decorated.

Being an only child to my mother who was almost 40 at my birth and the seventh and youngest for my dad at 44 years of age placed me in a protective world which forced me to live at times, in an environment empty of friends. I learned to make a playhouse out of a chicken coop and an old caboose. Next to Daddy and Mama, the "banty" hens became my most fervent audience.

This type of childhood developed in me a voracious appetite for creating — words and imagination, therefore making a firm foundation for a communication career.

We have a nation of people, young and old, dying to be heard! This book is written for the busy person who doesn't have the patience for "wasted words." The outline is basic and simple — wisdom at a glance. There is very little explanation or transition between section units. It is designed to let the poems and quotes speak for themselves. I would be especially pleased if the words arouse feelings for new ambitions as well as help you to verbalize the deep emotions you've never been able to express.

Open your heart with your eyes and as you read may you grow in self-esteem and communication skills and have a clearer understanding of all areas of your life — as a parent, student, employee, lover and child of God.

Put Feet To Your Dreams and Get Walking!

"FEARDOM" OF SPEECH

Chapter

1

So many people are suffering from the pain of swallowed words. We can tell total strangers on planes and buses our most heartfelt problems but we can't seem to talk to the people we love.

MY DEFINITION OF GOOD COMMUNICATION:

Say what you feel
    when you feel it
    to the person you feel it —
    with discretion and diplomacy!

Sometimes the best communicator may be the one who knows when to be silent.

Words of pain seem to slip out so easily I want to catch them before they fall on you.
Words can scar.
Words can inspire.
Words can change lives … and relationships.

Never write anything on paper you can't live with for a lifetime.

WORDS FOR RENT!

Here are some words for rent. Try them on for size:

"I love you but I'm mad!"
"Let's talk about it till we feel better together."

Give the people you love time to brew with their words.

Remember, what someone says to you at first may not be the problem. It's usually the last thing they say when they walk out the door that counts.

Everyone needs a "hollering" post — someone they can "holler" at and still be loved.

LOVE RELATIONSHIPS

Chapter

2

To be loved is to be liked from the toenails up — just the way you are!

Be the best self you can be before you give yourself to anyone else — then you love each other out of a choice and not out of a have to!

Scripts:

Men: Never say, "I'll call you," if you don't mean to!

Women: Never say, "Ask me out again sometime," if you don't mean it!

Start out knowing all the ground rules of a relationship instead of playing emotional charades with someone's heart! Never play games with gestures of passion.

Love yourself enough to be loved before you love.

The want for love sometimes gets confused when we put labels of love on the wrong people who don't feel our needs — just because we want someone to love.

Are you in love with love or just filling in the blanks with feelings you want to feel? If so, play it smart enough to face the facts before you commit a life to a wish.

HELP WANTED!

I want a relationship with someone who counts so that I can feel joy and pain and grow and become with someone, a we.

I want someone to walk with me along the road of life.

I don't always want to walk alone — but I need my own quiet time so I can look forward to our togetherness.

GOOD RELATIONSHIPS COME FROM LOVING THE RIGHT PEOPLE

People who bring out the best in you.

When you find someone you can be you with, and they still think you're great — you've got it.

We blindly stumble into love and bump into someone and say —

I think I love you
I think I love you too — duh.

To walk away from one you love, out of love, hurts more than staying in a relationship of destructive pride in a land of unquenchable thirst.

We're so afraid we'll never be picked again that sometimes we choose them because we think it's going to be our last chance.

The highest form of love is turning loose.

Photos by Ed Finley

*One of my

favorite times ...

getting hugs,

and talking

with my audiences

in small groups

after the program

is over.*

Photo by Elea Finholt

WHY NOT TO GET MARRIED

Chapter
3

This is not a chapter against marriage; but because of the high divorce rate caused by poor coupling and inappropriate hitching, I must write this section.

The illogical reasons people use to get married — let's look at some of them and test them in our relationships.

1. The Picket Fence Syndrome:

If you want a station wagon ... if you want a king size bed ... a 2000 inch color TV ... house and large dog and even your own set of tools and washer and dryer ... you may need to get married.

HOGWASH!

You don't have to have that to have a full life?

Don't live your life on hold, always waiting for "prince" or "princess charming."

Be the best self you can be before you give yourself to someone else. Then you love out of a choice and not out of a have to.

2. Don't We Look Good Together!

If you're so hung up on looking cute and impressing people plan a mock wedding. Rent a groom or bride with all the gowns, tuxedos and all the excitement. Invite your friends and have a big party. (They can even bring gifts). Then you can go home with all the loot but go home alone.

"Aloneness" isn't so bad. In fact, until you have encountered lying next to one you supposedly love and feel the loneliness, you don't really understand this step.

Don't get hung up with the tinsel. Remember the tenderness!

3. I Don't Want Him But You Can't Have Him Either Syndrome

Jealousy has forced many marriages.

Don't talk yourself into marriage!

I've seen divorced men and women fall for "little Johnny needs a mother and father."

Did you ever consider you need a husband or wife? I told a divorced father recently who kept falling in love with his son's babysitters, that if he wanted a cook, housekeeper and babysitter he should hire the servants and marry a woman!

You should be happy with so-and-so — they are so nice. Everyone likes them so much.

I say let everyone else marry them!

4. Waiting For The Tills!

Better to marry a diamond today than to sit on an old chunk of coal forever.

Get someone who comes "fully growed"!

Education work — don't take a sap to raise!

Watch out for "motheritis" and "fatheritis."

Feeling sorry for a potential spouse is not a good reason to marry.

Someday we'll be happy —

Today is tomorrow all used up.

If you can't enjoy today with all the sizzle and respect you want and need for this person — Start over — or wait awhile.

My dad always said you can't live on love and eat and sleep on a clothesline.

5. My Heart Beats With Every Toll Of The Cash Register!

Falling in love for money leaves you being bought and sold and not your own person — that's a high price for a life of servitude.

6. I Don't Want To Face The World Alone!

Many people get married out of insecurity and fear facing life alone. Be happy with your "aloneness" first!

7. The Storks Revenge!

I will not get into the case of talking about your moral decisions if you catch a case of pregnancy — if you should or shouldn't marry to do the right thing. First, we must accept the responsibility of our actions, of course if that had been done to begin with you wouldn't have gotten a "little" pregnant!

There are many options — face whether you love each other or not.

Is it forced love? A shotgun wedding as we call it in Texas. Sometimes the one who gets shot is the one who marries out of duty!

The revenge comes when you've decided to please everybody but yourself!

8. Too Hot Not To Cool Down!

You must have the physical chemistry ... but ... be sure you love each other past the bedroom, 'cause life can't be spent there ... and that's just really too bad!

9. Sacraments Don't Sanction!

Don't rely on the fact that you both have a strong faith to mean that the answer is yes! It may be meant for you to be prayer partners and not marriage partners. Faith is very important in a marriage but it needs respect and a reason for existence.

Just don't fall prey to talking yourself into marrying someone because of the spiritual level of communication that is mistaken as love — marriage love, not friend love. Know the difference. And if you are friends, love and marriage may be just around the corner.

Elizabeth Helvey and Brinson Strickland.

Photo by Holloway Photography

COTTON CANDY LOVE

We've lost our "we's"
Love today has become bodies touching
   like two faceless mannequins
      without sensitivity and vulnerability
   therefore not allowing growth of
   the "we" in relationships.

**Without even sharing our hearts and souls
   we've learned to bare our bodies.
I want a love that sees me past my cleavage,
   fat and wrinkles!**

We talk of sex like a road map to another state
   oh yes
      another state
         sometimes a state of emptiness
It's like a recipe
   we add a little kissing and a small pinch of love
      and, come on,
         we get what we cook up!

I Want To Be A 'We' In The Sunshine

Dear Lover —
I will love thee till I start feeling
   bad about me.
I will take each day as it is
   never expecting more than today's "clock full!"
Where did I lose me
   on what road
     with which traveler?
You have unlocked the real me
   I will never be the same
Now I can reach out and have confidence
   in my choice
I can say no
   and not feel belittled
When I say "yes" —
   I know it must be for real.
What is real?
   real is not a fabricated fairytale
     till death or change do us part!
Real is making today the most
   making time for me
Real is being important enough for me
   to notice you
     midst my never ending conquering journey.

I Will Never Love Empty Eyes Again

I feel bathed in sunlight
  my shadows are gone
    your shadow now holds a profile
      of me at your side

We hold hands
  we touch —
    we talk —
      we feel —
        we are —
And nothing can take that away
I take you as you are
  from the toenails up
All the while knowing
  that we are changing
    each second of each day
      together
I can't wait until next week
  to see what I'm like
    and to see your venturous growth.
Why have we remained hidden so long?
  accepting one half or less
    of what we want and need
      and never asking why —

I Thought I Was Following My Dream
But I Found Out It Was Chasing Me

How could I have felt so little of me
*   To allow my love to be so easily picked?*

Dance for me my love
  dance for me
    show me as I show you
      not my turn
        not your turn
          but our turn.
I want to be pursued as well as to pursue
What pleasure comes from frivolous "soap opera" games

Life is not a television show
We keep waiting for the show to end
  to go on to the commercials
    and they never come.
Please keep asking questions about me
  my loves
    my dreams
      my aspirations
        my reasons for being!
Your asking shows you care
  Your remembering what I say
    *and listening shows **we care**.*
I get so full of me when I'm with you
  I think I can fly

My treasure is deep and never been opened
    until now
        because I never saw myself clear enough
        to know my key —
What is my key
    my key is
        your sensitivity
            your chiseled words
                your rhythmic touches
Your looks that make me tingle all over
    when I feel I can't get close enough
Your patience and "boyish" spirit
    your visionary mind
        unbridled and never bound by fear
Your good judgement and
    perception to what most people never see
Your faith in God that shows
    in the sparkle in your eyes
        and your love that never ceases
to reach out to mankind like no one
    has ever done before.

Where did we lose ourselves
and fall for loves that felt like walls
and lived lives that tossed us to and fro
like a leaf on the water
getting soaked up by everybody else's
"want to's"
Where were our "want to's"
when they were handing out "want to's! ? ?"
Did I say I don't have any "want to's"
I don't need a turn?
I don't need anything
I'm just fine!
Did we totally negate ourselves
to be admired by others?
were we step-lovers to others
being cast away
like disposable hearts!
We reached out
and all we got
was COTTON CANDY LOVE
the kind that disappears in your hand
and never gets to your heart

Jayne Lybrand's Job Interview & Success Tips

1. Sit on the edge of chair, lean forward.
2. Observe the non-verbal cues in office.
3. Have a crafted commercial prepared showing your uniqueness and value.
4. Never make negative expressions or comments about a former employee.
5. Admit what you don't know, but show an eagerness to learn new things.
6. Never lie — about a former salary or negative previous work experience.
7. Dress the part — dressing for success is important. But remember you can put on a $500 suit and walk like a turkey and no one will believe in you.
8. Always have another interview scheduled. No one wants anyone no one else wants.
9. Get out when the "gettings" good. Leave them wanting to know more about you instead of telling them too much!

FAILURE IS A DRESS REHEARSAL
FOR SUCCESS!

Chapter
4

The whole world is teaching you how to succeed but the most important lesson you will ever learn is how to fail successfully.

The most successful people I know are good failures!

If we learn important lessons from our mistakes then our failures are never in vain.

The price of learning is a high price — but remember,

"what I've done for nothing is the price I've paid for knowing."

And no one can ever take that away from you.

ARE YOU LEARNING FROM YOUR DRESS REHEARSALS?

One Million Dollars and no/100
Career Development Certificate

Earns 100% Interest Daily in You!

_____

Is a Potential Millionaire

Jayne Lybrand Bank of Human Potential Affirmation List
(To Be Read Often)

- I'm valuable!
- I'm unique!
- I'm needed!
- I'm beautiful/handsome!

- No one can put me down!
- I'm proud of myself!
- I'm not afraid to attempt new things!

- I notice every beautiful thing in life, from a rose to a baby's toe!
- I will keep a list of my accomplishments and read them daily!

Non-transferrable — earned by merit negotiable in self-esteem cash!

34

SELF ESTEEM
AND DEALING WITH OUR FEARS

Chapter

5

The more I like me the more I can put up with you!

When you meet someone who doesn't like anyone and who feels the whole world is against them and that life in unfair, you're looking at someone who doesn't love themselves very much. When we love ourself it's amazing who and what we can put up with.

The people who can roll with the punches and deal with those who think differently than they do can put up with most anything because of their strong sense of self-esteem.

We need to be kinder to ourselves — to love ourselves more — to criticize ourselves less.

The fears of a relationship and verbalization of the random thoughts that travel through our heart and mind — can be best described through this poem. Although, written from a woman's point of view I feel men can identify with its emotion.

The Brink Of The Unknown

Oh!
   the complication of love!
      the search for that certain someone!
         the bliss of the unknown and new —
Crashing
   against the bareness
      of reality in the morning
The reality of what is
   compared to what one dreams
Moments that allow you
   to float away
      and tune out the noise
         and the humdrum and mediocre
The attraction of warm and unseen feelings
   that tug at your heart
      and your hormones.
The rush of sensuality —
   the magnificence of touch —
      the magnification of feeling —
         and obliteration of
           the ordinary.

Oh!
　　to stay there
　　　　safe in the arms of love!
A place that has no pain
　　and yet feels so safe
　　and protected
The needed pats and hugs
　　the enfolding and intertwining
　　　　that brings us so close
　　　　　　and yet so separate
　　　　　　　　in our own minds
Even through complete togetherness
　　one still holds the corners
　　　　of our minds that ask the
　　　　　　questions of acceptance
Is it worth it to risk and reach out —
　　to reveal
　　　　to say those worn out
　　　　　　yet censored words
　　　　　　"I love you?"

I have things so good
and safe
alone
but no pain
only the pain I inflict
not choiceful acceptance and rejection
of another who counts.
I am a self-contained woman
do I really need a man?
am I living in fantasy's requirements
and not the reality of me?
Oh yes I love thee —
but do I need one special man
can I limit my love
can I close out the freedom of choice
and resign myself again
to austere tradition and
blinders to the world.

No!
   I want it all or nothing!
I'm left with my world which I have created
      pushing away loves that others
         would have died for
            and hanging on at times to those
               whose kind comes cheap —
                  weird priorities of life and love.
I know of love
      but do I really know it?
         do I really want it?
            for that is the choice
               do I really want it?
Is my search an endless circle
      of patterning to destruction?
         for that is my destiny?
            or can I change my patterning
               and be open
                  to love for real?

I must make this choice!
I cannot flitter through life like a
   nervous hummingbird
      soaring close and
         when in arm's reach
            fly away —
Is it only the untouchable that looks good?
   do I desire only mirages of love?
When I look into your eyes
   I see you
      I see the you I think I see
         I the you you want me to see
            but do I really see you?
Across a crowded room
   our eyes meet like a magnet of souls
      a look that holds more feeling
         than a passionate encounter.

Bet on you!
You're the best product you'll ever have.

No matter what profession or what product you sell, your strong self-image and opinion of yourself is the best product you'll ever have.

In the job interview be confident.

Have a prepared, concise, original commercial for yourself — a few sentences crafted in a way that describes your strengths and uniqueness.

With regard to your future employment: If you don't believe in yourself — they don't need you.

Employers are looking for self-motivated people, not people who apologize for their very existence!

In love relationships, if there is someone you want to meet, walk up to them and say, "I'm a little nervous. I don't quite know what to say. I've been wanting to meet you. I don't want to make a fool of myself — but here I am!"

Be yourself. If others can't deal with the real and vulnerable you then you don't need them!

The following poem has been written out of many years of listening to accounts of traumatic experiences that are usually never talked about. Although it is written from a woman's point of view, anytime I read it during a speaking engagement I have men in the audience who tell me they feel the very same feelings represented here.

I Have The Right To My Own Body

I have the right to my own body —
  love cannot be forced
    it must be felt.
Oh the pain of having your physical being
  taken with gestures of passion
    intended for any convenient body.
I am not to be taken lightly —
  I deserve respect
    and thoughtfulness
      and the right to my own choice to give.
I must give out of a choice
  and not a have to.
Wild hands and kisses
  ignoring my feelings
    and lack of acceptance.
Being trampled on by
  a nameless monster of passion
    without a face
      only begging for starving hormones.
It stops
  when the tickle stops and all you have
    is the response
      and the feeling of unworthiness
        and being used.

I will not
be used again —
hear me if you want to be
real lovers
let us come to you
and not be taken
without being asked.
So you steal a feeling
In turn
you have lost the joy
of a potential discovery
of another's thoughts
dreams
words
and touches.
Quit stealing away in the night
love yourself enough to wait
until you get what you deserve.
A warm loving woman who
chooses you
of her own volition
without votes that are bought,
coerced or won
through intimidation
and words that say one thing
and actions that say another.
The pain of incongruent behavior
compared to
the memory of a tender,
growing relationship
that allows me
to give you more
than my body.

SUCCESS TIPS I WANT TO TELL YOU

Chapter

6

Lessons I've Learned The Hard Way:

1. Don't be like everybody else.

Everybody that has ever been great has been a sound and not an echo. Be the original. As soon as you start feeling the real you come out — look at it — talk to yourself — be proud of your uniqueness. Don't be clones of everyone else!

There is a stage in parent control when we think being opposite of what your parents or authority figures think really means we're individuals. There's nothing so great with being opposite. In fact it takes guts to stand next to someone and agree with them if they are right!

2. Incompetency will follow you the rest of your life!
Learn to deal with it.

I'm really tired of nice incompetency! It could be your boss someday! However, it's those nice incompetent people you can't get rid of. It you are going to be incompetent at least be a little "ornery!"

3. Do what is not being <u>done</u> — first.

If you do do what is being done, learn to be a little bit better than best — change in some way that shows your creativity and originality!

4. Learn to face your fears.

Behind every fear stands a potential joy waiting to be won by conquering that fear.

Real cowardice is never really trying at all!

5. Quit living for what everybody else thinks!

Live for what you think.

Be proud of your opinions and thoughts — nourish them — get lost in the comfort of thought and imagination.

6. Learn to deal with your own aloneness!

It worries me about the average young person today. They all say, "entertain me — where's the TV set — do you have a radio — do you have any magazines — where's the phone — well do you have anything to eat — entertain me!"

Learn to enjoy your own company and not panic when you're left alone.

Aloneness

Too much time seems to fall on me —
   I say take it back
      I don't need anymore time.
I don't know what to do with what I've got!
Time and emptiness closes in on me
   and chokes me
      time strangles me still —
How
   do I face it
      without my friends, activities or business?
My telephone
   and my letters
      become my best friends
         The joy of going to the mail box is
            the highlight of my day.
Eating becomes a dread formality —
   I gobble down my food
      standing up —
         why sit down at a table alone?
I'm drawn to sleep at an earlier hour —
   it helps ease the pain of my aloneness.
      The "mindless" television shows
         help me escape
            until the commercials wake me up to
            the reality

               of my aloneness again.

The repetition of the hands on the clock
    shout the same hours passing so slowly.
        I've looked out every window
            in hopes of a new adventure outside —
                only to be left with visions
                    of falling leaves
                        and squealing passing cats.
How can I stop time and make it my friend
    the warm comfortable friend I need so.

**The more happiness I find in solace
the more happiness I find in life.**

Oh, could it be
    the facing of another night or day
        is not so frightening anymore?
            could it be I've begun to read
                and get lost in my memories
                    and future plans?
To enjoy the sensory pleasures again
    the smell of coffee brewing
        the warmth of a fire
            the comfort of an old blanket.
The familiar noises of my house
    that lull me to sleep
        with the sameness of predictable existence
            I can now deal with.
Oh! time —
    Oh! aloneness —
        you are my friend
            and I have so much of you
                to look forward to
Now that we're both on the same side.

7. Look for wisdom in all the wrong places.

Sure, education has wisdom — but I've paid my dues and lived out my sentence. But learn to listen to the people who serve America. They're the ones who can teach you. Go to nursing homes and ask questions of those who've been around the block — a lot of times.

Don't just live through the years! Let life pass through your ears!

My precious and wise mother,
Ruby McHugh Brannon

8. Learn to be lazy on cue.

Relaxed living is a breeding ground for creativity and will make you burst on the work scene "raring to go!"

Cracking Your Own Whip!

Crack your own whip —
    If I do this diet, I'll lose weight
        feel the **burn**
If I go to this program,
    I'll stop smoking.
If I join this group,
    I'll control my drinking.
If I find my magic Pied Piper of bad habits,
    I will appear slim, beautiful and undaunted
        by nasty haunting addictions.

Please Somebody, Do All This For Me!

I can't do it myself
    or can I?
Not to put down credible and marvelous
    national self-help organizations that have
        changed so many people's lives
But
    the real change begins with me
        my own ability to admit my problem
        and make a choiceful action
            to begin its correction.
I must learn to crack my own whip.
    I've waited too long for it to be done for me.
When someone else does it
    I change temporarily
        until I fall back
        into old ways

My ways must change
　　help me to look
　　　　at me and face my fears
　　　　　　to conquer the albatross on my shoulder.
I, as everyone else,
　　have my own haunts.
Only I can erase my own ghosts
　　by cracking my own whip.
　　　　instead of waiting for it to be done for me!

I must be in control and
　　allow my life to be lived
　　　　by me
　　　　　　not to me.

As I share my heart, the audience
feeds me with their smiles.

Photo by Ed Finley

10. Have a reason for being.

Life without a purpose is sheer existence.
Show me a selfish or greedy person and I'll show you someone who hates life and most people.

11. Remember, you don't step up stepping on!

12. Your value is not in who you know — it's who wants to know you.

Qualities Of Successful People

1. Know themselves
2. Riskers
3. Think big
4. Implement dreams
5. Act — follow through
6. Keep Promises
7. Have a good self-image
8. Can say **no**
9. Keep seeking new ideas and constantly keep discovering themselves
10. Are rarely threatened by others thoughts, words of touches
11. Don't sleep, eat or drink their troubles away.

PARENT TALK

Chapter

7

It seems that all parents have gone to the same school of parenting when it comes to communication. Let's call this school "The Parental School Of Stereotypic Behavior!"

After speaking, at times to audiences of 20,000 young people a month across this country, I hear the same complaints aimed toward their parents. This chapter is aimed toward parents who want to know how to communicate better with their children. Here is a compilation of students "most hated" phrases and philosophies that we as parents seem to use most frequently. These theories/comments guarantee poor communication with our children.

Let's Get Rid Of:
I told you so's!
All parents have gone through the rain,
the sleet, the snow to school up hill both
ways!!!

I've done it all for you — the martyr syndrome (said while they rhythmically pat their chest with the flat of their hand).

And, our all-time favorite, **someday you'll be sorry!**

The greatest gift we can give our children is to turn loose of them long enough to allow them to walk life's pathway alone and know they can when we're not around.

Hug them till they squirm!

Oh Mother! REALLY!!

Do your kids have the "Oh Mother" syndrome? Are they at the stage where everytime you say something witty and "with it" their response is: Oh Mother, really!

Do they make you feel two inches high with their:

    Eyeball rolls

    Sighs of disgust

    Elbow thrusts

If that's it mother, you're in the "Oh Mother" scene.

State Of The Young Address

BE IT THAT FROM THIS DAY FORTH we will listen with our hearts and not just our ears;

That we are slow to advise and wise in our direction;

Help us to put up with each other when it seems no one cares;

Give us the arms that have no boundaries —
    eyes with 20-20 insight —
    feet with dreams that never grow weary —
    gestures that speak our truth without being
    hidden by plastic smiles of pretense.

Voices that utter the simplest feeling with care and diplomacy, Bearing in mind the sharp-edged swords of words when not tempered by thought.

Hearts that have no walls to judgemental relationships

and love that teaches us to turn loose!

Help us give our young people our greatest gift — that of the right to go after their dreams with all they are and have, because we were the role models that showed them it is possible.

Jayne and daughter, Elizabeth

Photo by Bob Jones

KID TALK

Chapter

8

Art Of Pouting

Here's a tip on the downward lip
When you get your mouth going sideways —
Pout, buddy, pout
If you're going to do it, do it good —
There's no such thing as a half pout.
A pout can win you pity or peers
depending on the size of your pucker!

Oh Mother, r-e-e-a-a-l-l-l-y! (Said with a growling sound during the final sound on the word, really, while you roll your eyeballs in the top of your head, shuffle your feet and fold your arms like you're bored to tears!)

Get on with it. Are you through? (This is one of their most popular replies.)

You don't understand me! (Said while stomping their feet up the stairs to their room as they slam their bedroom door and turn on their stereo as loud as possible!

If you want your parents to listen to you, try doing this when they are talking to you:

1. Sit on the edge of your chair.
2. Lean forward
3. Move your head left to right ... slowly (thinking, for shame, for shame, for shame. Then turn your jaw to the left and nod up and down **slowly,** pause, hold that pose and count ten seconds.)

Most parents will stop talking and start admiring how much you have matured!

Also, it gets a new car at Christmas if done right. (where applicable)

May I share with you a poem my daughter Elizabeth wrote for me when she was very young:

My Elizabeth

Only Mammy And Ibby Will Understand

There are some people in the world
   that would do anything
      for someone they loved —
There are even people who
   devote their whole life to
      help a person they love —
         they're not the important ones.
The ones who really make a difference
   are the ones that first
      have a life of their own
And they are willing to reach beyond that
   to hold someone in their arms
      to wipe their tears away
         to say I'm behind you all the way.
They can because
   they are their own person first
      who knows their own capabilities
         and is willing to share them with
            the person they love the most.

Elizabeth Helvey

Everybody's Child

Young people today don't see
　　the positives about themselves
　　　　they get hung up
　　　　　　on their negatives.
They are afraid of
　　rejection
　　　　attention being drawn to them
　　　　　　being different.
They want to be accepted by the "norm"
　　whatever that is.
Everybody's child
　　everybody dictates their everything
　　　　everybody's doing it!
Who is everybody?
　　I'll walk, talk and dress the way
　　　　"everybody" does
　　　　　　to try to fit in.
I worry about you when life ceases to
　　entertain
　　　　when you're left alone with
　　　　　　four walls void of TV sets and stereos.

If you could be
the guy or gal
on the magazine cover
"picture perfect"
Would you still not love yourself?
would you still
feel fat and ugly
dumb and stupid?

How can I make you see your inner beauty
  the beauty I pray someone
    will marry in you someday?
How can I teach you objectivity
  and the ability to deal with failure?
What someone else feels about you
  is not how you are!
You wait and allow others
  to dictate your self worth.
Please stop listening to Everybody!
  Your opinion
    is what really matters
      how you feel about yourself
        during your complete aloneness
You are beautiful! You are handsome!
In our world
  the imperfect noses —
    unusual hair —
      rare voices —
        different words and philosophies —
          always seem to lead.
Why do you run from who you are?
  face your "differentness!"

Be the sound
  and not the echo.

I guess to know me is to know my daughter Elizabeth. She was born with her mind made up — strong and gentle — quieter than me — but my biggest fan.

Please let me share with you a part of a book she wrote. May I introduce Jayne Lybrand, through my daughter's eyes at 12 years old.

Although she's younger than 12 in this picture, this is a hug I will never forget from my little girl.

This Lady I Know

You see there's this lady I know
   I've never met anyone like her
She's different from anyone
    and is loved
      and respected by
         everyone who knows her
She has more "children" than anyone
   everyone of them is
      going to be successful because of
        her guidance and love
But there's this one small girl
   who loves her
    more than anyone else
You see — this girl is I
   I live with the neatest lady
    you could ever meet
      This lady I know
        has always been there to help me
We've really had it tough!
   we've lived through everything!

Everyone always said
  I was the image of her
    God
      my wish
        my only wish
          is to be her image
As rough and tough and stern
  but more sensitive and caring than anyone
    God ever made
Now I'm beginning to understand
  everything she's done for me
She can be anything she wants to be with
confidence
  now she can do what she has dreamed of
    how could this lady I know
      accomplish all of this?
She's never turned me down when I needed her
  and never will
I love her more than anything
There's knowing how much she loves me
  that's so important!
There's knowing she would do anything for me
  there's this feeling I have for her
    that means so much
There's no way
  I could ever say enough
    about this lady I know
      you see
        she's my mommy and
          I'm proud
            to be her friend!
I
  Love
  Her!

Elizabeth Helvey

There's always a reason for our pain.
Sometimes we can't see it and sometimes we never do.
We live it out instead of learning it out!

My Elizabeth, all grown up
Photo by Bob Jones

"TAPESTRY LIVING"

Chapter

9

I call this section *Tapestry Living*

You know how the back of a tapestry is all stringy with frazzled edges and colors overlapping without any visible signs of beauty. It's like life. Our lives are like tapestries. We don't know what's going on sometimes or how to deal with our problems or better still, why we even have them!

The Master of Life knows and allows us to see ourselves step by step.

All the pieces do fit together with the right seamstress or artist!

The following poem was written on a plane. Being in the air about 20 hours a week I spend a lot of time on planes. Therefore that is my best time for creative thought. As I gazed out my window one day I wrote this poem and subtitled it Flight 109.

The Beauty And Glory Of God's Creation

No two clouds or people
    are the same.
As I gaze out my window
    to see the clouds
        I want to catch the specialness of each one
           before I lose its sight!
             I'll never see that same motion-wisp
           of glory again.
It's like people
    look and search for the specialness in everyone.
      God planted a special seed
        in each one of His children —
It's for us to discover it
    water it and let it grow and bloom.
But it helps if the love of others
    can help us see it in ourselves
        and give us strength
      and walk hand and hand on this earth.
It's like our friends are extensions of God —
    to hold our hand when we fear,
      to comfort us when we fall,
        and to love us just the way we are.
Wake up and look for the diamond within you!
    Only you can allow
        the inner giving gift to become a reality
      for that, my friend
        is the miracle of living

To discover ourselves
  like our Heavenly Father
    already knows
      and allows us to see ourselves
        like He wants us to be.
It's like when we finally see ourselves
  we're right under our nose
But without our clarity of ourselves we live
  in darkness and fear.
When we unmask our beauty
  we soar free
    and grow so fast
      only God can keep score.
**Every time I think I know myself I find a new
part of me I never met before!**

Put Feet To Your Dreams And Get Walking!

Break out within this shell of fear
    peek up over the sides
        and say to the world
            I'm here!
Stand up on your tip toes
    and look over the hurdles of life
        and even though the top
            is only a dream of what is out there —
Keep stretching
    keep reaching
        keep hoping
            keep loving
                keep hugging.
Don't let negative creatures rain on your parade
    don't let anybody hold you down,
        but most of all don't let you hold you down.
Because you my friend can set a barrier
    to joy — to growth — to success
        that has no antidote.
Don't build cobwebs around your life —
    stand in the sunshine —
        move out of the shadows!

If we could say what we feel
and not hold back what we will
until it explodes in unharnessing anger,
it's so much easier to talk it out
and not let it brew.
Here's my challenge to you —
Take your life off hold!
and say it to those you love
and say it to those who might hire you
and say it to those who sneer you
But most of all
say it to you!

for availability for speaking engagements,
cassettes and books contact:
Jayne Lybrand Associates, 817-267-9086
P.O. Box 1187, Bedford, Texas 76095

Books — $7.00 plus $1.00 for postage and handling